LIBERTY FIRST:

The Path

to

Restoring America

By KrisAnne Hall

i

ISBN-10: 1477690913

ISBN-13: 978-1477690918

DEDICATION

To all those dear patriots who put *Liberty First!* To those who realize that the battle will never be over and that their sacrifice is worth the cost. To those who recognize the great worth of the generations and millions yet unborn and have therefore made an eternal pledge to give Life, Fortune and Sacred Honor. To those who recognize the great price paid by the generation and millions yet past who have already given Life, Fortune and Sacred Honor to secure one of the greatest gifts ever given to mankind by a Merciful and Gracious Creator, the Giver of Life and Breath. It is for His honor and glory that we give our full devotion to His cause – the cause of Liberty. This great battle before us is not simply a battle for America; it is a Kingdom battle. Choose this day who you will follow. As for me and my house, we will serve the Lord.

KrisAnne Hall

CONTENTS

ACKNOWLEDGMENTS

Thank you to all the America-loving, grass roots groups that have given me opportunity to share the message of Liberty. To those who have donated, bought books, let me sleep in your home, bought me a hotel room or plane ticket, filled my gas tank and prayed for me. It is because of you that my small part in this fight continues on.

Thank you to my family for their support and for the many times they have accompanied me on my trips up and down the road to proclaim Liberty to the remnant and for the many times they have stayed behind.

A special thanks to all my sisters in the battle. You Esthers, Mercys, Penelopes and Abigails. We've laughed, we've cried, we've danced, we gone absolutely **Beach Nuts.** I love you all.

KrisAnne Hall

Prologue

America's Very Survival Is At Stake

I have been traveling the country for the last two years, teaching people the true history of the founding of our nation. I do this because I believe two things: one, that God has placed a call on my life and two, those who do not know their history are doomed to repeat its mistakes.

On several occasions I have been able to teach rooms full of high school and middle school students. At the end of the presentation, I am always encouraged by the fact that they really get it. They really understand what 99% of our politicians don't, that our nation was built with the purpose of securing the blessings of Liberty for our posterity, for ages and millions yet unborn.

By the end of the presentations, my heart is so uplifted by their enthusiasm and patriotism, I could storm the doors of tyranny all by myself with a dull butter knife. But, I also shudder when I think of what **we** have done to them, what **we** have given away on their behalf.

On one occasion, I had to stop my teaching and tell them that I had to apologize. I suddenly realized the mess that **we** left behind for them. I was weeping in front of a room full of teenagers, and I could not stop myself. I looked into their eyes and realized, through our ignorance and our negligence, we have very nearly condemned them to purchase back a gift that was **given** to us; **a gift that we were supposed to secure for them, not require them to secure for themselves.** I got angry for a minute, but that anger made me even more resolved. I told them,

"Don't you dare use our negligence as an excuse. You go out and fight for what is rightfully yours. If the government tells you that you cannot speak, does that make you mute? If the government tells you that you cannot assemble, does that imprison you? If the government tells you that you cannot freely worship God, does that silence your soul?" To each question, with wide eyes, they responded "no." I told them, "Then do not be silenced, do not be imprisoned, and let your soul cry out. Because I promise you, from this day forward, I will do everything I am both humanly and

supernaturally able to do to take back ground for you. I will do everything I can to make sure that you have the Liberty that was purchased for you, that belongs to you, that you are entitled to have as a glorious gift from God. I promise!"

I took an oath when I joined the military to support and defend the Constitution. I took an oath when I was sworn in as an attorney in the state of Florida to support and defend the Constitution. I took the same oath when I was sworn in as an Assistant State Attorney for Florida. I know that these oaths NEVER expire. That day, with those future leaders of America, I took another oath, one that will never expire, one that I will fight to keep to my very dying breath. This is why I do what I do. This is why my family and I travel all over the country. This is why I teach. That is why WE do what WE do. For Liberty. For America. For our children.

We are in a battle for the hearts and minds of Americans. We are in a battle for our future. We are in a battle to reclaim the culture. The further continuance of one of the grandest displays of Liberty is at stake – the future existence of America as we know it.

Nearly half of the American populace has been successfully brainwashed into embracing the principles of statism and collectivism. We elected a President in 2008 that spews collectivist ideology to the ignorant masses on a daily basis, and they willingly swallow it, HOPING it will somehow CHANGE their circumstance.

No longer are the high offices of our land used to motivate the people to ingenuity and self-reliance, but the greatness of government is extolled and dependency is encouraged. The old Soviet mantra of "hate the rich" is now a daily headline and the fundamental platform of the Democrat party.

The statist in the White House swept to office with the promise of fundamentally changing America. Somehow we lost sight of the fact that the fundamentals are not what's wrong with America, but rather, the fact that we have strayed so far from them. Declaring that the Constitution was "fundamentally flawed," the aspiring leftist telegraphed for all who would actually listen that he did not believe in or agree with the fundamental principles and framework that has made America the greatest bastion of Liberty and opportunity that mankind has ever known. He has brought with him nefarious cohorts who declare Communist leaders like Mao Zedong and brutal murderers like Che Guevara to be their heroes. He has filled our highest offices with sympathizers to radical Islam and racist groups like the Black Panthers. He has frightened hordes of businessmen out of the marketplace. He has engaged in cronyism and apparent kickbacks to his donors, all while spending America into oblivion on the backs of taxpayers and their children.

Make no mistake; we are in a fight for our very survival. We must restore America or be lost forever. We must restore America or be doomed to live as tributary slaves to tyrants. We must restore America by putting Liberty First!

KrisAnne Hall

1. Keep the Proper Perspective

One of the most important keys to restoring America to its greatness and to the principles of Liberty is that we must keep the proper perspective. WE THE PEOPLE are the power and we will not stop until we have righted this ship. The federal government is intended to be limited and WE THE PEOPLE are the power and the foundation of the Republic. The government is our beast to rule over, we are not serfs toiling to keep the government fed.

Conservatives, Libertarians, and Constitutionalists are often characterized as wanting no government. This straw-man argument, a.k.a lie, is what simple-minded people say when they do not want to address the issues. Those who want no government are anarchists, that's not us. We want a LIMITED government as defined by the Constitution and as explained by our founders.

Our founders did not make the federal government sovereign over the people or the states. The 9th Amendment makes it perfectly clear that all rights belong to the people, enumerated or not. The 10th Amendment makes it clear that aside from the powers "delegated" to the federal government, EVERYTHING ELSE belongs to the people through their states. It is clear that the framers purposefully and intentionally created a federal government that was to be limited in power and scope. Extremely limited.

The Federal government was only delegated very limited powers. James Madison said those powers were limited primarily to external objects and named them specifically as 1)war, 2)peace, 3)foreign commerce and 4)negotiations.

"The powers delegated by the proposed Constitution to the federal government are *few and defined*. Those which are to remain in the State governments are *numerous and indefinite.* The former will be exercised principally on external **objects, as war, peace, negotiation, and foreign commerce**; with which last the power of taxation will, for the most part, be connected. The powers reserved to the several States will extend to **all the objects which, in the ordinary course of affairs, concern the lives, liberties, and**

properties of the people, and the internal order, improvement, and prosperity of the State." Fed. 45 (emphasis added)

Simply speaking, if it is not war, peace, negotiations and foreign commerce, the federal government is not supposed to be involved in it. Period. What that means for us, is that the federal government has no business whatsoever in our health care, or in our businesses, in our schools, or in any other aspect of daily life!

Over the years, through an absolute dearth of true Constitutional teaching in the government schools and in law schools and through the replacement of precedent over the intent of the founders, we have allowed our courts to stray far from the original limitations and purpose of the Constitution. Our federal government was designed to be our national representative to the foreign world, a representative of the country in foreign relations. Because we lived in a world where nations where led by Kings, Czars, and Emperors, we needed to have a way that all the states could have a unified voice for negotiations and commerce. During the Articles of Confederation, our federal government could not collect taxes or even compel the delegates to show up to work and do their job. The federal government was attempting to make agreements with foreign nations and was defaulting on these agreements because they had no authority to enforce them equally throughout the states, and the states themselves were suffering the greatest consequences. As reported in The Address and Reasons of Dissent of the Minority of the Convention of Pennsylvania to their Constituents, written December 12, 1787, this very point was addressed.

"It was found that our national character was sinking in the opinion of foreign nations. The Congress could make treaties of commerce, but could not enforce the observance of them. We were suffering from the restrictions of foreign nations, who had shackled our commerce, while we were unable to retaliate: and all now agreed that it would be advantageous to the union to enlarge the powers of Congress; that they should be enabled in the amplest manner to regulate commerce, and to lay and collect duties on the imports throughout the United States."

We must keep the proper perspective. We have three branches of government. All co-equal, deriving their power from the people and restrained by the Constitution. This means the Supreme Court is NOT the ultimate arbiter of the Constitutionality of a law. The Supreme Court is 1/3 of the federal government, with no more or less power than the other two branches. It is **the Constitution** that is the Supreme law of the land, not the Justices of the Supreme Court, and all decisions, even ones made by the court must stand before the ultimate judge, the Rule of Law in the Constitution.

The Constitution was written and ratified by "an act of the whole American People" as Thomas Jefferson declared in 1802. Its purpose is to "secure the blessings of Liberty...to our posterity". To secure that Liberty, "governments were instituted among men", not over them, and "derive their just powers from the consent of the governed." Our founders gave us a government dependent upon OUR consent, not the will of the Supreme Court, the President or Congress. Our founders knew that since Liberty belonged to us, we would be the only ones suited to determine when "any form of

government became destructive to those ends."

Because of this lack of Constitutional understanding that

permeates even our highest branches of government and our

highest courts in the land, we have strayed far from the intent of

our founders. I dare say, James Madison himself would barely

recognize the government we have today. Actually, maybe he

would, because it looks a great deal like the one he and his patriot

brothers and sisters pledged their lives, fortunes, and sacred honor

to declare independence FROM and ultimately defeat in the name

of Liberty.

One principle in our Constitution that has been warped beyond

recognition is the "general welfare clause." Our founders never

intended for the "general welfare" clause to mean the "limitless

power" clause. Madison explains in his 1792 argument against

federal subsidies that the general welfare clause was not meant to

expand the power of the government beyond its limitations, but to

describe the purpose of the power delegated within strict

confinement of those boundaries. This was not just his opinion, but the opinion of ALL who drafted the Constitution.

"I, sir, have always conceived -- I believe those who proposed the Constitution conceived -- it is still more fully known, and more material to observe, that those who ratified the Constitution conceived -- that this is not an indefinite government, deriving its powers from the general terms prefixed to the specified powers -- but a limited government, tied down to the specified powers, which explain and define the general terms." James Madison, On the Cod Fishery Bill, granting Bounties 1792

Madison was very simply explaining that the clause "common defense and general welfare" was not meant to be used as a justification to expand the power of the government beyond its limitations, but that the clause simply states the purpose of the powers which had been enumerated within the Constitution itself. How we have flipped this nation on its head! We have allowed our government to take the description of the purpose of its power and turn it into its very power. This gross and despicable distortion of our founder's intent is not without consequence. We cannot have it both ways; it is either a limited government or one completely without limits. In fact, we learn from our founders, that the Federal government was not even supposed to have the power to tax and subsidize, unless it is attached to the four areas Madison mentioned. Madison knew such misinterpretations would unleash Pandora's Box and that Liberty would collapse under the weight of such a philosophy. "There are consequences, sir, still more extensive, which, as they follow dearly from the doctrine combated, must either be admitted, or the doctrine must be given up." James Madison, On the Cod Fishery Bill, granting Bounties 1792

Although our founders may not have known about all our great technological advancements and the needs of our modern day society, they knew that human nature remains the same. They did not have to know where we would end up, because they knew where they had come from.

"I have but one lamp by which my feet are guided; and that is the lamp of experience. I know of no way of judging of the future but by the past." Patrick Henry St. John's Church, Richmond, Virginia, March 23, 1775.

With astounding foresight Madison describes what a totalitarian, nanny-state America, that ignores and distorts Constitutional meaning would look like. "If Congress can employ money indefinitely to the general welfare, and are the sole and supreme judges of the general welfare, they may take the care of religion into their Own hands; they may appoint teachers in every state, county, and parish, and pay them out of their public treasury; they may take into their own hands the education of children, establishing in like manner schools throughout the Union; they may assume the provision for the poor; they may undertake the regulation of all roads other than post-roads; in short, everything, from the highest object of state legislation down to the most minute object of police, would be thrown under the power of Congress; for every object I have mentioned would admit of the application of money, and might be called, if Congress pleased, provisions for the general welfare." James Madison, On the Cod

Fishery Bill, granting Bounties 1792

I blush to think how Madison might have reacted to the

atrocious opinion issued by Chief Justice Roberts, who argues the

polar opposite of what Madison expresses here. Madison and the

framers knew that if the government would become more than

they had intended, it would control the very lives of the people, and

we would be reduced to "tributary slaves."

The current use of the general welfare clause, outside of the

intent of our founders, is unconstitutional and it will create slaves of

freemen. It is irrelevant how any modern court has determined

otherwise. If the courts have failed to follow the direction of the

drafters of this contract, they have failed to follow fundamental

principles of law and their decisions are void of authority.

It is up to the people to keep the proper perspective on these

principles and on the foundational intent of our founders, because

it will be up to us to correct the government when they get it all

wrong. Hamilton articulated this responsibility very well in

Federalist Paper #33. "If the federal government should overpass the just bounds of its authority and make a tyrannical use of its powers, the people, whose creature it is, must appeal to the standard they have formed, and take such measures to redress the injury done to the Constitution…"

Keeping the proper perspective means we must work to restore the limitations of government. The states and the people must stand against federal overreach. Our governors and state legislatures must take up their duty as independent sovereigns and declare to the federal government that we will not comply with unconstitutional laws.

The breach of Constitutional boundaries is the source of the corruption, as told by the warning, now prophecy, of John Adams in his inaugural address of 1797.

"[If the government is] Negligent of its regulations, inattent[ive] to [the people's] recommendations, … disobedience to its authority, … soon appeared with their melancholy consequences-- universal languor, jealousies and rivalries of States, decline of navigation and commerce, discouragement of necessary manufactures, universal fall in the value of lands and their produce, contempt of public and private faith, loss of consideration and credit with foreign nations, and at length in discontents, animosities, combinations, partial conventions, and insurrection, threatening some great national calamity."

Until we force our current government to work within the boundaries set by our founders: war, peace, negotiations, and foreign commerce, we will suffer all of the corruption that Adams foresaw. We have to be dedicated to the principle that these limitations are more than just recommendations, our recommendations are more than just rhetoric, and separation of powers must be viciously protected by all parties! This is the disease of our nation and we must cure the disease or it will be the death of Liberty.

We have allowed the powers of the federal government to expand far beyond what our founders intended, to the point that their warnings have become prophecy. We cannot allow this to continue. For the sake of our children, we must reign in this unconstitutional proclamation of power. We must once again hear the warnings of our founders and heed them, or suffer the inevitable consequences. Keeping the proper perspective in the responsibility of the people, the limited role of the government, and the restrictions on power placed on each branch is a vital part of restoring America by putting Liberty First.

- Remember That We The People Are The Power.
- The Government Belongs To Us; We Do Not Belong To The Government.
- The Constitution Is The Supreme Law Of The Land; Not Any One Branch Of Government.
- The Federal Powers Were Intended To Be Few And Defined.
- Securing Liberty Falls To The Sovereign States And Ultimately To The People.
- We Are The Final Check And Balance.
- We Are In This For The Long Haul.

2. EDUCATE BEYOND THE ELECTION

One of the most important items we must accomplish in restoring America is educating beyond the election. We are not just attempting to change out the occupants of political office; we are attempting to change the culture. It is likely that many of us will hold and attend fewer meetings after an important election, particularly if "we win." We are prone to speak less about the Principles of Liberty and abandon our duty to educate our children and fellow citizens. A similar mistake was made after the House takeover in 1994. Conservatives won a great victory, and then many rested on their laurels. We did little to effect long-lasting change, because a significant education component was not part of our strategy. The Heritage Foundation continued its part, but its focus was still toward the halls of power, rather than on impacting the minds of everyday Americans.

Elections are not the end-all, be-all of how we the people govern this nation. Campaigning and winning elections is not enough to secure Liberty in America. If we are to secure the America we want for ourselves and our posterity, we must continue to educate beyond the election.

Our Founders believed that only a truly informed and educated people could maintain Liberty. Sam Adams said in a letter written to James Warren on November 4, 1775,

"...when People are universally ignorant, and debauched in their Manners, they will sink under their own weight without the Aid of foreign Invaders."

All of our focus and resources can't be centered on elections and politicians; we have to reach the people. Remember that politicians are apt to tell us what we want to hear and not what they truly believe. We can't afford (and I mean that quite literally) to put the politicians in office and then spend the entire term wrestling with them to do what's right. We have to make a difference long before that happens.

I believe that pastor S.G. Winchester in 1856 was correct in saying that, *"Families are the appointed nurseries of both Church* *and State. **They are to furnish civil society with virtuous and worthy members**, and the church with active, useful, and devoted Christians."* (emphasis added)

Therefore, we must educate the nation, the households that will be providing the future politicians, so that the candidates take the right principles *with them* into the capitols and into the courts.

Understand that we are not just working for today. In fact, terms of office are temporary; rarely does a Congress look the same from session to session. But, the education portion of our strategy aims at more permanent ends, to fix a "Liberty First" perspective in the minds of the people, rooted and grounded in the Constitution and its History.

We have long been negligent in teaching the Constitution and its principles. Many who profess to be committed to the Constitution simply do not have the foundation necessary to live up to that promise. We have seen the consequences of this time and again, even after the 2010 "conservative" win. If we fail to teach truly conservative and Constitutional principles to our future political candidates, we will quickly lose any progress that we have made in restoring true republican (not the party) government. We cannot take one step forward and two steps back. Our grass roots restoration must maintain a steady momentum.

This tyrannical administration has had a rather "happy effect," in that, it has united the patriotic sentiments of like-minded citizens and has driven us to be more Constitutionally aware than we have ever been. We must keep moving. If we lose momentum, I tremble at the thought of what will have to happen to get us moving again.

Keep meeting. Keep teaching. Educate our fellow citizens. And most especially – get the right information into the hands and minds of your children. After each election, it is the juniors and seniors in high school who will vote in the next election. We need to target the young, the high school students, the college students, as well as then the current voters. Teach! Teach! Teach!

"Train up a child in the way he should go and when he is old he'll not depart from it." Proverb 22:6

KrisAnne Hall

I am only one of many educators involved in the mission to enlighten the minds of Americans. I plan to do my part as long as I can. I am not the smartest. I am not the best writer or speaker. What I am, is a person who has the distinct honor of traveling the country and teaching the history of our Liberty and the principles that make America an exceptional nation.

I have recently been extended the honor of joining the Federalist Society's speakers list, and I look forward to being able to speak at Law schools around the country. It is a common misconception that attorneys automatically understand the Constitution by virtue of having graduated law school.

We must remember that lawyers are simply college graduates who have passed the bar, and judges are those law school graduates who have gotten a promotion. Unless any of those students has independently sought out an understanding of the Constitution, they are probably devoid of any real understanding of its principles. Most law schools simply DO NOT teach the Constitution. At best, they teach Constitutional Law, and there is a

BIG difference between that and the Constitution. Many times the Constitutional Law classes distort and destroy a proper understanding of the Constitution or shift its authority to courts and precedent.

Once again, if we put Liberty First and teach our children in the home, then they will be inoculated against any disinformation campaign waged against them under the guise of "education." Eventually, we may be able to retake our Law schools with professors who actually know and believe in the principles of Liberty that are contained in our founding documents.

I also have the privilege of teaching grass roots groups, local political parties, candidates, politicians, judges and lawyers and, best of all, middle and high school students. I put an average of 6,000 miles per month on my car and many more miles in the air. Oftentimes, I spend more than I take in to keep the effort going. But, we all believe that our nation and our children are worth the effort.

I personally believe that if we can wage this war with information and activism while we still have time, then we can avoid the bullets, but we must be committed to the long haul. Mercy Otis Warren wrote on December 29, 1774, "America stands armed with resolution and virtue; but she still recoils at the idea of drawing the sword against the nation from whence she derived her origin. Yet Britain, like an unnatural parent, is ready to plunge her dagger into the bosom of her affectionate offspring. But may we not yet hope for more lenient measures!" We didn't get here overnight; we can't get it back in one night. We must be resolute, and we must never stop praying for the "more lenient measures."

One of the primary weapons we have in this long fight to restore the minds of Americans to a Liberty First perspective is education. We must change the culture in our homes, in our schools, in our communities, in our churches. We must make our history and the principles of Liberty part of our lives again. This knowledge has nearly vanished from the minds of Americans. We must reintroduce it, so that we are anchored in it. So it guides our decision making. Teach your groups. Research it. Own it. Spread it.

We can't keep placing and replacing politicians and never get to the root of the problem. We will never solve these great issues if we do not recapture and recreate the American mind. Let's give this our utmost attention. Let's support the educators and become educators ourselves – through and beyond the election. We must teach the principles that put LIBERTY FIRST.

- Educate.

- Make Liberty First Principles Part Of Our Daily Lives.

- Do Not Stop At Elections.

- Do Not Start At Elections.

- Research/Learn From The Founders' Own Writings.

- Disseminate. Teach.

- Support A Teacher.

- Be A Teacher.

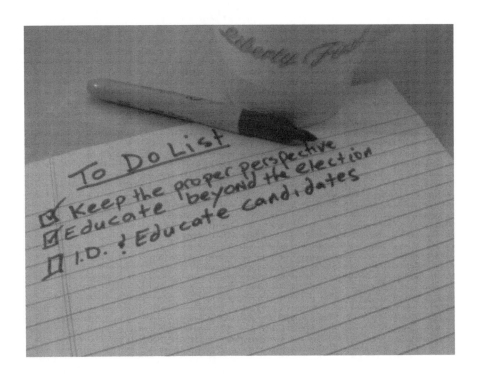

3. IDENTIFY AND EDUCATE CANDIDATES

While education is vital to our long-term success, we must also be active in the political trenches. Since we are a republican form of government, one of the most important things we can do is identify appropriate representatives for the people and ensure that they are properly educated on the Constitution and the Principles of Liberty. It is of the utmost necessity that the representatives we choose have a Liberty First perspective.

We must be careful not to make our selection based on a motive of fear or to choose representatives who do likewise. Sure we must defend our nation. Sure we must strive to maintain peace and security, but we must resolve that violating the Constitution is not the answer to fighting terrorism or any other threat.

As I write this there is a steady "domestic militarization" taking place in America. Even the EPA apparently now has armed officers. We have drones being requisitioned to patrol the skies of America. DHS has grown into a massive and monstrous bureaucracy armed to the teeth. In the name of fighting terrorism, they raid family farms and ranches, viciously putting down the menace of raw milk and the threat of homegrown chickens and their deadly eggs.

As TSA gropes grandma and searches suspicious baby diapers, I can't help but think that we are to blame. We have chosen and elected politicians without giving one thought to what they may know (or may not know) about the fundamental principles of Liberty.

Patrick Henry's burning question is still fitting for our day. In the St. John's Church in 1776 Henry asked, *"What is it that gentlemen wish? What would they have? Is life so dear, or peace so sweet, as to be purchased at the price of chains and slavery?"*

Henry affirms that life and peace are two of the most valuable possessions a people may have. But at what price? Will we volunteer for a life of bondage and slavery to keep our lives? Will we thrust ourselves into shackles and chains simply to garner peace and safety for ourselves?

"Forbid it, Almighty God!," he declares, *"I know not what course others may take, but as for me, give me liberty or give me death!"*

Patrick Henry was declaring that without liberty even our greatest achievements and most valuable possessions are nothing but bondage. Without liberty; our jobs, our healthcare, our government, and yes our national security will be purchased with bondage and slavery. That is why I believe that rather than asking what "free services" they are going to secure for us, it is absolutely vital to demand that our representatives have a "Liberty First" perspective, so they don't sell us into slavery with their "good intentions."

We need representatives who will not compromise first principles, which means they must first know what those principles are. I believe that we must require our representatives to have the training necessary to support and defend the Constitution. Simply reading the Constitution or professing attendance in a Constitutional law class is not sufficient. We must find a set of programs suitable for the training of those defenders of Liberty, and then make that training a job requirement.

Liberty First!

The power of the government is derived from the people, therefore the people must require their representatives to be proficient in the application of the principles that make our Constitution relevant and our nation exceptional. Our grassroots groups need to hold Constitutional training courses; invite all the candidates, local, state, and national and then ONLY endorse those who attend AND show proficiency in our founding principles. Do not accept excuses for not participating in this training. I have heard them all: I'm too busy campaigning, I already know the Constitution, I don't need to attend this class... I say, make our endorsements contingent upon the proper training, and then the candidates will make it a PART of campaigning.

We should be working toward an election day where the standard for electing a candidate is NOT that he is simply better than the other guy. We are all sick of holding our noses and voting. We must educate our candidates so that the choice is a Constitutionally-qualified candidate who believes in AND understands the fundamental principles of Liberty.

Every company you've ever worked for gave you training. Why in the (excuse me) don't we give our representatives training?!?! I worked as a plumber in college and had to be trained before my boss would ever let me touch a toilet! Our representatives are putting their grimy, untrained hands on one of the greatest gifts ever given to mankind by a Holy God – the gift of Liberty!

Additionally, we need to choose candidates who are morally fit, which means we must first PRODUCE candidates that are morally fit. If we do not get our own houses in order and live before our children with integrity and teach them to do the same, we will be forever doomed to pick "the lesser of two evils" when we get to the voting booth.

Samuel Adams made the connection between the necessity for a moral people to have moral representatives. In a letter to James Warren on November 4, 1775, Adams said,

"There are Virtues & vices which are properly called political. Corruption, Dishonesty to one's Country, Luxury and Extravagance tend to the Ruin of States. The opposite Virtues tend to their

Establishment. But there is a Connection between Vices as well as Virtues and one opens the Door for the Entrance of another. Therefore Wise and able Politicians will guard against other Vices, and be attentive to promote every Virtue. He who is void of virtuous Attachments in private Life, is, or very soon will be void of all Regard for his Country. There is seldom an Instance of a Man guilty of betraying his Country, who had not before lost the Feeling of moral Obligations in his private Connections."

Simply put, a person's private life must match his public life, and his actions must support his rhetoric. Let's stop listening to sound bites and campaign speeches. Take a look at records. Is this man or woman a person of integrity? Have they kept their word? Does their record reflect who they are now, or are they reinventing themselves to get elected?

I am astounded at the people we've elected who claim to be true conservatives, or who are Tea Party darlings, yet every single time the Constitution has been on the chopping block they have voted the wrong way. They bark and bluster about spending. They wrap themselves in the flag and pay homage to the military. Yet, on the one thing that makes America what it is – Liberty – they seem to be as ignorant as a day-old infant. While claiming claim with "fire in their belly" to be conservative, they voted to gut the 4th, 5th and 6th amendments in NDAA 2012. They voted to make your right to assemble a federal crime in HR 347. They continually support the expansion of federal police powers in the name of fighting terrorism and have no problem diminishing Constitutionally-protected rights to do it. And when challenged, it always boils down to one argument – "it's necessary." "We have to do this because _____ " (fill in the blank). As William Pitt said in the House of Commons, 1783,

"Necessity is the plea for every infringement of human freedom. It is the argument of tyrants; it is the creed of slaves."

We are supposed to be more cautious and deliberate in our evaluations and not be swayed by bullying or bombast. Our founders expected us to look into the past practices of our future representatives to verify they are who they say they are, and that they understand the principles that they are supposed to support and defend. That is precisely why the founders established that the president had to be at least 35 years old and Senators 30 years old. They wanted us to have "time to form a judgment" and to ensure that these prospective representatives would "not be liable to deceive."

"As the select assemblies for choosing the President, as well as the State legislatures who appoint the senators, will in general be composed of the most enlightened and respectable citizens, there is reason to presume that their attention and their votes will be directed to those men only who have become the most distinguished by their abilities and virtue, and in whom the people perceive just grounds for confidence. The Constitution manifests very particular attention to this object. By excluding men under thirty-five from the first office, and those under thirty from the second, it confines the electors to men of whom the people have had time to form a judgment, and with respect to whom they will not be liable to be deceived by those brilliant appearances of genius

and patriotism, which, like transient meteors, sometimes mislead as well as dazzle." [John Jay, Federalist Paper 64]

Say what you mean; do what you say; be who you are; and support and defend the Supreme Law of the Land. I stand by my statement, **"If you have to circumvent the Constitution to do your job, you are a traitor and a criminal."** We don't need liars and pretenders. The cowardly and covetous need not apply. Let's identify the right candidates based on the right principles. Let's take an active role in giving them those principles, starting in the home, then to the neighbor, then to courthouse and statehouse. We must accept nothing less than LIBERTY FIRST!

- Choose Reps Who Will Not Compromise First Principles.
- Choose Reps Who Have Proven Their Understanding Of First Principles.
- Choose Reps Who Have Proven Their Character.

- Make Them Answer To Us.

- Focus On Liberty First, Not Services Or Security.

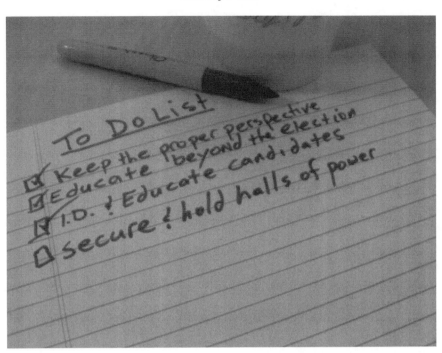

4. SECURE AND HOLD THE HALLS OF POWER

GET-OUT-THE-VOTE

Having chosen the proper people with the right principles and with a demonstrated ethical and moral foundation, we must work to place them in office. We have to be active in our get-out-the-vote efforts. As I said before, we can't rest on our laurels. The enemy doesn't take a vacation (of course that axiom doesn't apply to the Obama family however). John Philpot reminded us in 1790, in his speech before Privy Council, that there is no vacation for the patriot who loves liberty and wants to maintain it.

"It is the common fate of the indolent to see their rights become a prey to the active," he says. "The condition upon which God hath given liberty to man is eternal vigilance; which condition if he break, servitude is at once the consequence of his crime and the punishment of his guilt."

We must maintain our community contacts and have structures in place to activate the voters. This means contacting voters, informing voters and getting them to the polls. This is the nuts and bolts of securing our political offices , you have to get to the people one on one. Expand the voting base by reaching people with the truth and get them to vote, that's how we secure these offices. There are great tools out there, like PoliticalGravity, to get this done. True The Vote and The Abigail Adams Project can be of value in this effort, as well Mark Adams' Voter Fraud Initiative at the Save America Foundation, since we must combat voter fraud and be informed about the candidates. It doesn't help to get all of our voters to the polls only to be outvoted by Donald Duck and dead people.

Do NOT Neglect Local Politics

As part of our efforts we cannot have too narrow of a focus – we must control National, State AND LOCAL offices. One of the greatest dangers I have seen in our struggle to gain and hold the political institutions is the neglect of LOCAL politics. National politics is sexy and attracts all the media attention, but it is at the local level that we have the most power, and it is local politics that affects us most immediately.

It is from the LOCAL political bodies and corresponding agencies that the greatest attacks on our property and liberty have come. This is the primary ground where the ominous-sounding UN Agenda 21 has operated. This is also why so few people know anything about this threat ; its mechanisms are local, therefore it attracts almost no media attention. So when you mention it, you sound like a tinfoil-hat-wearing kook. Sadly, its destructive tentacles are everywhere.

I have to put a fence around my own yard if I expect to keep intruders out. Our local offices are our fence when Federal protections fail us. Conservatives MUST occupy our school boards, county and city bodies, clerks of the court, District attorney's offices, and sheriff and police departments. The local level is the last line of defense, but sadly it is one of the first areas of infiltration by the enemies of Liberty.

We must also control our local state houses, because our governors and state legislators are supposed to be our guardians against Federal encroachment. Madison wrote on June 8, 1789:

"...because the state legislatures will jealously and closely watch the operations of this government, and be able to resist with more effect every assumption of power than any other power on earth can do; and the greatest opponents to a federal government admit the state legislatures to be sure guardians of the people's liberty."

How many of our state legislators understand their primary job description, in the eyes of our founders, is to protect their people and their states from federal encroachment? That's why we must educate our candidates and representatives. That's why local is so important. As I send this to print, SCOTUS has just issued two disastrous rulings that diminish Liberty. The Arizona ruling declared that the Federal government is sovereign over the states, and the "healthcare" ruling declared that the federal government is sovereign over the citizen. It is now the obligation of the states to stand in defense of the Constitution and protect its citizens from this unconstitutional attack. If we ever needed a modern example of why local and state offices cannot be neglected, we have it now.

Break The Addiction

We must acknowledge that the number one obstacle that prevents our state representatives from adequately defending us from Federal abuse is our addiction to Federal funds. If we do not restructure our lives in such a way that we can operate without "strings-attached money," then we will never win this battle. If you want your politician to do the right thing, then you better be willing to be self-sufficient. We will never have the Liberty we want if we do not break our addiction to the Federal Drug.

Our founders warned us time and time again about giving in to the ever expansive reach of the federal government in the name of provision. Our dependence on the Federal government has led to a massive expansion of entitlement programs which are leading us like a runaway train into national bankruptcy. I am afraid, however, that our national debt problems are simply a reflection of our personal debt problems. The best way to strengthen America, would be for Americans to get out of debt and stop living beyond our means. We want everything now and we want someone else to pay for it. If we do not wean ourselves off of debt personally and nationally, it will be our undoing. Debt is slavery, plain and simple.

Debt limits your choices and puts you under someone else's

control, and eventually they come to collect.

Secure Congress

Finally, If we truly want to press forward with a Constitutional,

prosperity-promoting, America-centered agenda, then we must also

control both House and Senate. Having a Constitutionally sound

Congress can be the greatest defense for Liberty that we can have

in American government. It can guard against a tyrannical

President or a rogue Judicial system. It can also give support to an

executive agenda that takes America in the right direction.

Once we have secured the House and Senate we must keep it.

In 1994 Republicans enjoyed sweeping victories in the Congress.

They eventually lost those gains due, in large part, to big-

government RINOs carrying out business-as-usual, establishment

politics, all while claiming to be true conservatives. In 2010 we had

one of the most sweeping victories in the House of Representatives.

Yet, many of the so-called conservatives of 2010 have been a great

disappointment, but we can't give up. I believe that we hold on to

Congress by electing and re-electing Constitutionally minded representatives, who will not negotiate away our Liberty for any reason. It is a *Liberty First* principle that will get people into office, and it's a *Liberty First* principle that must maintain their office. If they stray from that single focus, it is time to replace them. Why should we hold our current representatives under lesser standards than our founders held themselves. In a letter to Edward Carrington on January 16, 1787 Thomas Jefferson made this observation,

"If once they (the people) become inattentive to the public affairs, you and I, and Congress, and Assemblies, judges and governors shall all become wolves. It seems to be the law of our general nature, in spite of individual exceptions..."

If Thomas Jefferson characterized himself as having a propensity to become a "wolf," then we must always observe our representative continually and make immediate corrections whenever necessary. Holding on to the House and the Senate does not mean its "our" party that is a majority. It is no longer enough simply to be elected as a Constitutional conservative; we must

require the appropriate votes, regardless of party, personality, or

career achievements. We secure and hold those in Congress who

are firmly attached to the Constitution and have made a

conscientious determination to support Liberty at all hazards. I am

reminded of a song in one of my favorite classic musicals, *My Fair

Lady.* The female lead sings to her language teacher, "Words,

words, words, I'm so sick of words, sing me no songs, read me no

rhyme, don't waste my time show me! Never do I want to hear

another word, there isn't one I haven't heard, say one more word

and I'll scream. Show me." Yes, Eliza, I feel your pain. Congress, no

more words, SHOW US! Then we may let you keep your jobs!

Often when candidates tell us one thing but then practice

another, many voters get discouraged and withdraw from

participating. "They are all corrupt, so why should I vote?" That is

not the proper response. "Of the people, by the people, and for the

people" defines our obligation. *Of the people* means the

representatives came from us, they are a product of our households and communities. We cannot withdraw, because at the heart of the problem is us. Like it or not, we are the root cause. *By the people* means that we are the ones who operate this government – we cannot withdraw and leave the system to run itself (that's how we got into this mess). *For the people* means that it is all for our benefit and, most importantly, for the benefit of our children and generations to come – we cannot withdraw, because we have a great responsibility and obligation to those who cannot take action for themselves. If we do withdraw we will become a nation "*of* politicians, *by* state governments, *for* Washington, DC." Therefore, to secure Liberty for ourselves and the rising generation, we must put forth every effort to secure and hold National, State and Local offices with citizens dedicated to putting LIBERTY FIRST.

- Get Out The Vote.

- Pay Attention To Local Offices.

- Fight Agenda 21.

- Secure The State Capitols

- Win Congress.

- Run Good Candidates For Every Office.

- Become Self-sufficient.

5. PURGE AND RECAPTURE THE GOP

I believe that an essential element in the restoration of this nation is the restoration of the GOP. Conservatives have to seize our local party committees, as well as our state and national party committees. We have been foiled time and again because the party apparatus is filled with unprincipled power brokers who care only about gaining and maintaining power. Principled candidates who will not compromise for personal gain are a threat to the establishment political machine. The sad thing is that when we are talking in terms of "establishment" there is no difference between the republicans and the democrats. They are not really party loyal but **power loyal**, and the GOP establishment has abandoned the principles that made this party the choice of Frederick Douglas, Martin Luther King Jr., and Ronald Reagan. (Albeit, the more I study the policies of Reagan the more I wonder about some the globalization and the undermining of American sovereignty.)

Liberty First!

To the establishment, the Tea Party movement feels like a revolution when in fact it is a *restoration* of the principles that should make the GOP the Constitutional party. We must purge this establishment mentality from the GOP so that those who are Constitutionally minded will have the opportunity to prosper and grow into the experienced, Liberty minded conservatives necessary to secure the blessings of Liberty for our posterity. Having an "R" behind your name is not an indication that someone is a "conservative." I wonder if that indicator was not abolished with the likes of Teddy Roosevelt. Nonetheless, since it does not seem to be possible to remove ourselves from a party system anytime soon, we must RESTORE the GOP to Constitutional principles, elect representatives that profess and maintain those principles, and immediately eliminate those who do not.

One place to begin in this restoration process might be for people to stop sending money to the RNC or even their state party offices. Perhaps, we should make a concerted effort to individually support candidates that exhibit those valued principles, regardless of party. When I was called by my state party office this year and asked to donate, I declined. I made this decision because I did not see the "party" holding its representatives accountable. I asked the kind lady on the phone if she could tell me whether the party was denying party support to any incumbent based upon votes that are contrary to the principles of the party. She said they do not. You see, the party does not police itself – or perhaps it does. If you have an "R" behind your name and you are a RINO, you will still get party support.

Until the party as a state or national movement starts requiring the manifestation of the principles they profess and denying support to those who do not follow those principles, I will continue to make those judgments as an individual. If we hold back enough funding, the principles of capitalism teach us that the GOP may have a wakeup call, and we will be well on our way to restoration.

However, I think the best approach is to take over the party apparatus. We must fill our local Republican Executive Committees with *true Constitutional* conservatives. Once we have a majority in these committees, we secure the positions of leadership. This allows us entry into the state-level delegations. If we do this statewide, county by county, then we can have a majority at the state level and secure leadership there. Then onto the national level. This has already been happening in many places. I read recently of several liberty-minded patriots that made their way, just as I've described, into the highest levels of GOP leadership.

Let's face it; if you do not operate within the party apparatus, your power to influence the outcome of the political process is diminished. However, we would do well to heed the warnings of our founding fathers on the dangers of party influence. One of the greatest opponents to parties was George Washington. Once again, Washington's warnings in his farewell address sound like a prophecy and if we do not take it to heart, we will never restore the values of this nation.

"The alternate domination of **one faction over another**, sharpened by the spirit of revenge, natural to party dissension, which in different ages and countries **has perpetrated the most**

horrid enormities, is itself a frightful despotism. But this leads at length to a more formal and permanent despotism. The disorders and miseries which result gradually incline the minds of men to **seek security** and repose in the **absolute power of an individual**; and sooner or later **the chief of some prevailing faction**, more able or more fortunate than his competitors, turns this disposition to the **purposes of his own elevation**, on the **ruins of public liberty**."
[emphasis added]

The GOP failing to turn in the right direction, may force our hand. Rather than reform it, we may have to abandon it, en masse, if we want to put LIBERTY FIRST.

- Don't Blindly Support The Parties.

- Support Liberty First Candidates.

- Take Over The GOP Political Apparatus.

- Expose/Get Rid Of RINO's.

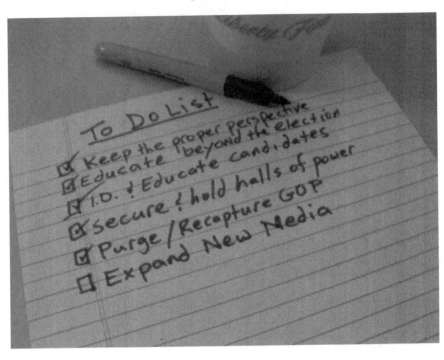

6. Expand New Media

One of the most influential forces in this present restoration effort has been "New Media." New Media includes the internet, the blogosphere, Facebook, Twitter, talk radio and the like. Probably the biggest pioneers of the New Media have been Rush Limbaugh in the talk radio world and Andrew Brietbart in the blogosphere and grass roots journalism.

Rush has been a thorn in the liberals' side for decades. Since his talk radio debut in 1984, his pioneering efforts have spawned thousands of talk jocks and laid the foundation for the modern day talk radio juggernaut. Why talk radio works and why it is conservative is simple: it includes the people. There is no public voice or input in the mainstream media. There is no feedback from the people on the nightly news. There is no immediate public voice in newspapers or magazines. There is no input or challenge to what is being disseminated in the mainstream media; therefore, it remains decidedly slanted toward leftist, statist ideology – matching the worldview of it owners and editors. In contrast, when the people are involved, the stance will tend toward conservatism. First, because conservatism is supported by the truth; secondly, because most Americas are truly conservative. That is why liberal talk radio cannot survive unless it is supported by taxpayer dollars. That is also why mainstream media is losing its viewership left and right and has been taken to the woodshed by conservative, new media. It is no wonder that those who cannot stand on the truth hate the free expression of it. Justice Oliver Wendell Holmes, Jr. remarked on this very concept in the Supreme Court decision in *Abrams v. United States* , 250 U.S. 616 (1919).

"If you have no doubt of your premises or your power, and want a certain result with all your heart, you naturally express your wishes in law, and sweep away all opposition. To allow opposition by speech seems to indicate that you think the speech impotent... when men have realized that time has upset many fighting faiths, they may come to believe even more than they believe the very foundations of their own conduct that the ultimate good desired is

better reached by free trade in ideas -- that the best test of truth is the power of the thought to get itself accepted in the competition of the market, and that truth is the only ground upon which their wishes safely can be carried out."

Liberals do not desire to compete in the free marketplace of ideas; they simply wish to silence the competition. We must continue to win the hearts and minds of people by disseminating the truth, and new media provides that opportunity like never before.

One of those opportunities is through the internet. The internet blogosphere provides a response to the monolithic, leftist voice in the echo chamber known as the mainstream media. The late Andrew Breitbart was one of the most impactful figures in this area of new media. Starting as an editor of the Drudge report (another foundational block in New Media) and then helping Arianna Huffington launch her site, Breitbart launched his own empire. With all his "BIG" sites and his internet journalism, he sparked the ire of seemingly every liberal in the known universe. I once heard Andrew tell a crowd that the key to making the biggest impact is "be petty." Andrew was funny, brilliant and a tireless and fearless warrior and we must follow on in his footsteps. Every patriot should have a video camera and be a citizen journalist. Andrew used citizen journalism as well as anyone to expose the hypocrisy and nastiness of the Left. He believed this was a battle "between good and evil" and he used new media to "shine light on the darkness." The great thing about video is even if you have no talent to write, you can hold a camera.

Something Andrew Breitbart loved, along with millions of other activists, is Social Media. Social media, like Facebook and Twitter, allows super-fast dissemination of information that is not filtered or controlled by some editorial board or other "overseer," for the most part.

One of the difficulties in the late conservative awakening is that a large portion of the engaged citizens are older and less adept at some of the technologies like Facebook. We must continue to expand our social media networks. It may sound silly, but the more "likes" a page has the more influence and reach it has (same principle with Twitter). We need to get as many conservatives as possible connected on social media.

If you feel yourself a techno misfit, I encourage you to attend a Right Online conference held by American's for Prosperity. There is no better grassroots techno training available. I have AFP to thank for much of what I know and understand about these new media outlets. It was at the Right Online conference that I got hooked on Twitter. It's also where I became friends with Andrew Breitbart and Katy Abrams. I met Michelle Malkin and scores of other great patriot activists. AFP does fantastic work at keeping the citizen network connected, motivated and engaged. (P.S. don't email me your Koch Brother comments, I am an independent patriot and I will use whatever tool I need to fight for Liberty – and my message will not change!)

Make no mistake New Media is having an impact and the mainstream media is scared to death. If they had their way they would use the power of the government to shut New Media down.

Just listen to the constant complaints and attacks from the left

against FOX News or Faux News as the liberal hacks like to say.

Conservatives are willing to let the issue be settled in the free

market place of ideas; the left always want to bring the power of

government to bear and shut down any discourse or opposing view

altogether.

A columnist for the Washington Post recently telegraphed his

fear of open discourse in New Media. He says it will be nearly

impossible for a President (read: Obama) to win a second term

"because the fracturing of the media makes it hard to push a clear

message."[1] I say, Amen! Clearly this "journalist" is ignorant of the

media's primary responsibility to be a watchdog against the

government not to be the government's lap dog. Translation: you

in the New Media will be THE REASON Obama loses – and the MSM

HATES IT!

---

[1] *Can any president succeed in today's political world?* Chris Cillizza, Washington Post June 17, 2012 (http://www.washingtonpost.com/politics/can-any-president-succeed-in-todays-political-world/2012/06/17/gJQAPBFIjV_story.html?hpid=z2)

John Adams said "Without the pen of the author of Common Sense, the sword of Washington would have been raised in vain."

You citizen journalists are THE power that will check this out-of-control government. You are the pen of Thomas Paine. The sword wielded by the American people in the ballot box will be raised in vain if the pens of the modern day Paines stop writing. We need conservatives in the field of Journalism, citizen journalism and professional journalism. -It would be nice if there were a prominent Journalism school somewhere that wasn't liberal- We need more tweeters, more Facebookers, more talk show hosts, more bloggers. Keep writing the op-eds. Keep publishing books, newsletters, magazines, and pamphlets. Information is power and we must dislodge the liberal stranglehold on the media (I dream of a day when New York is not the media hub in America). As I heard Michelle Malkin say recently: "It's not the Mainstream Media versus New Media, its right media versus wrong media."

The God-given right which is protected by the First Amendment, can be lost without active participation. This right is protected by its very engagement - we use it or we will lose it.   At

least one of our founders felt that it was the most important right

protected in the Bill of Rights. Daniel Webster said, *"If all my*

possessions were taken from me with one exception, I would choose

to keep the power of communication, for by it I would soon regain

all the rest." On the other hand, Patrick Henry who was also a great

orator, pretty much said you keep your speeches and I will keep my

guns. Nevertheless, if we fail to put this "first liberty" first, we will

soon lose all the rest.

- Write. Publish. Speak.

- Start A Blog

- Start A Radio Program.

- Go To/Start A Journalism School

- Open A TV Station

- Start A New Liberty First, Media Empire!

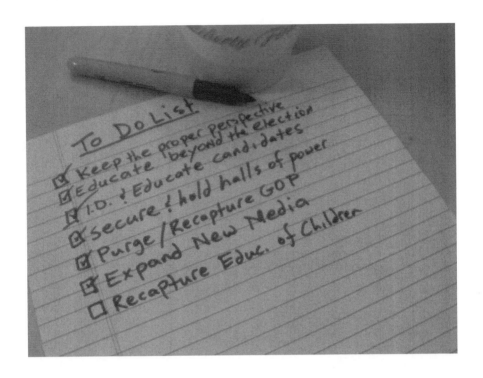

7. Recapture the Education of Our Children

This current point ties into every single previous point. This is not only a continuation of education beyond the election, but also how we will produce future Constitutionally minded candidates, secure and maintain a Liberty-focused Congress, continue to purge the GOP, and establish and expand our new media outlets. Those we need to educate first and foremost are our own children. The American education system at every level has been gradually and thoroughly hijacked by leftist ideologues. One of the greatest contributors to America's march toward Marxism is the brainwashing of generations of America's children. America's children have been kidnapped by the enemies of American Liberty. Our educational system has become concentration camps of brainwashing and Marxist programming.

Our students are not only NOT taught the Constitution and the Principles of Liberty, they ARE constantly indoctrinated that America is the source of all that is evil in the world — America's founding documents are flawed, its founding fathers were bigoted

oppressors, its values antiquated, its free market system

destructive. If we are to correct this menace, we must know the

people and principles upon which our educational system has been

built. The problems with education are not class size, not funding,

not teachers. We miss the point by focusing on teachers, their pay,

their benefits, their tenure. The problems are deeper than this. In

truth it's not a teacher problem; it's a system problem, and its roots

run deep. The "dumbing down" of American education has been

occurring since the 1800's [2] This process has been a steady march

toward "globalist" thinking, with the establishment of a global

Marxist and Humanist society as its goal. Consider the facts:

- Wilhelm Wundt in 1832 was the founder of Experimental

  Psychology and the Force behind its dissemination

  throughout the western world. His foundational theory

  became the <u>basis for teacher training</u> for over 150 years: he

---

[2] The best presentation of these facts can be found in a book titled, The Deliberate Dumbing Down of America by Charlotte Iserbyt. She was dismissed under Reagan for exposing this poison. You can download her book for free.

taught that children were nothing more than a stimulus response mechanism – nothing more than animated meat made up of neurons and electrochemical reactions.

- Edward Lee Thorndike, in 1903 was a professor of education and writer of 507 books on the methods of teaching which helps form the basis of teacher training and philosophy today. He said that children could be equated to "rats, monkeys, fish, cats, and chickens" animals that simply needed to be programmed.

- John Dewey, heralded as the father of modern education, is actually the father of progressive education. He wrote the book Psychology, it was the most widely-read and quoted textbook used in schools for teachers in this country. Dewey taught that the primary commitment to literacy was the greatest problem that the American school system faced. He believed that the goal of education was to make the student a productive member of the collective, to stamp out individualism and self-reliance. Look at some of the quotes from this father of modern education and one of the signers

of The Humanist Manifesto:

"The plea for the predominance of <u>learning to read</u> in early

education seems to me <u>a perversion</u>."

"Undue premium is put upon the ability to read at a certain

chronological age…the entertainment plus information

motive for reading conduces the habit of <u>solitary</u> self-

entertainment"

"We violate the child's nature and render difficult the best

ethical results, by introducing the child too abruptly to a

number of special studies, of reading, writing, geography.

The true center of correlation on the school subjects is not

science, nor literature, nor history, nor geography, but the

child's own <u>social</u> activities"

"The mere absorption of facts and truth is so exclusively an

<u>individual</u> affair that it tends very naturally to pass into

selfishness. There is no obvious <u>social</u> motive for the

acquirement of learning; there is no <u>social</u> gain therein."

- G. Stanley Hall (1844-1924), John Dewey's professor believed that education was simply to provide skilled workers, the less able to engage in independent thought the better. He taught that it was better to be illiterate, "the knowledge which illiterates acquire is probably a much larger proportion of it practical. Moreover, they escape much eye strain and mental excitement and other things being equal are probably more active and less sedentary"…"illiterates escape certain temptations, such as vacuous and vicious reading. Perhaps, we are prone to put too high value both upon the ability to read and the discipline involved in doing so."

So, it's no surprise that we graduate our high school seniors at a 50% illiteracy rate, having this as the very foundation of America's educational system. Like a scene out of George Orwell's 1984, even our parents clamor for an education system that simply provides job skills. Generations now DO NOT recognize communism when they hear it and even beg for it themselves.

What about the actions of our own government in corrupting our education system? The General Education Board was incorporated by congress in 1902; endowed by John D. Rockefeller, Sr. The purpose was to set up an educational laboratory to experiment with the very educational system Wundt, Thorndike and Dewey proposed. The Director of this congressionally-established organization, Frederick Gates said, "In our dream, we have limitless resources, and the people yield themselves with perfect docility to our molding hands. The **present educational conventions fade from our minds**; and, unhampered by tradition, we work *our own good will* upon a grateful and responsive folk." (emphasis added)

The 1917 Congressional Record of the US Senate published this statement: "The General Education Board was authorized to do almost every conceivable thing which is anywise related to education, from opening a kitchen to establishing a university, and its power to connect itself with the work of every sort of educational plant or enterprise conceivable will be especially

observed."

The movers and shakers in education at the time were

delighted and greatly influenced by the outbreak of Communism in

the Russian world. In 1918, in an issue of New York World, William

Boyce Thompson, Federal Reserve Bank Director and founding

member of the Council on Foreign relations made the following

observation: "Russia is pointing the way to great and sweeping

world changes. When I sat and watched those democratic conclaves

in Russia, I felt I would welcome a similar scene in the United

States."

Dr. Augustus Thomas, Commissioner of Education for the State

of Maine stated to a conference of world educators in 1927, "If

there are those who think we are to jump immediately into a new

world order, actuated by complete understanding and brotherly

love, they are doomed to disappointment. If we are ever to

approach that time, it will be after patient and persistent effort of

long duration."

Those shaping our educational foundations had a decidedly globalist view. John Eugene Harley, Law Professor at Harvard published a book called International Understanding in 1931 and made this statement: "And the builder of this new world must be education. Education alone can lay the foundation on which the building is to rest. Plainly the first step in the case of each country is to train an elite to think, feel, and act *internationally*." (emphasis added)

President Herbert Hoover in 1932 appointed a research committee on recent social trends, not approved or funded by Congress, but an Executive action underwritten by the Rockefeller Foundation. No report was ever made to Congress or to the people. It assembled the largest community of social scientist ever assembled to assess the social condition of the nation.

At the same time the NEA, federally chartered in 1906, created the Educational Policies Commission in 1932 and published a document titled Education for all Youth with the following goals for solving problems in the educational system and working toward the new progressive education:

- Federal programs for health, education, and welfare combined into one bureau

- Head start programs

- Getting preschool children into the system

- Youth services through a poverty program

- Removal of local control of political and educational matters "without seeming to do so"

- Sex education

In 1942 the American Federation of Teachers published a book titled America, Russia and The Communist Party in the Postwar World "If this war is to be followed by a just and lasting peace, America and Russia must find a way to get along together...the UN, including America and Russia, is the only agency that can establish such peace." The UN Charter became effective on October 24, 1945 with the US Chamber of Commerce was a prime mover in establishing the UN. The United Nations Educational, Scientific and

Cultural Organization(UNESCO) and its mandate for international intellectual co-operation had already been working under a League of Nations resolution on 21 September 1921. America now has taxed funded UN charter school all over the United States. They feed our children a daily dose of globalist indoctrination, banning the pledge of allegiance and substituting the UN Charter for the Constituion.

In 1958 right in line with the General Education Board, Thompson, Thomas, and Harley, Eisenhower signed the first set of agreements with the Soviet Union, which included an education agreement. Agreements just like this have been signed by every single president since Eisenhower.

There continues to be a concerted effort on every front to make our children believe they are global citizens, which will undermine and eventually destroy the sovereignty of the United States.

Even our children's heroes are going global: On May 2011 Superman relinquished his US citizenship. In the 900th Issue,

Superman says, "I intend to speak before the United Nations tomorrow and inform them I am renouncing my US Citizenship".

Now we have Race to the Top, the established and printed purpose of this program, as stated in national education directives is to transfer loyalty from the family to the government.

We cannot wait to fix the public schools; we must start NOW at home. THEN fix the public schools by taking over the local school boards. Elect representative who will restrain or eliminate the Department of Education. Fire representatives who attack parents' rights to educate their children, like those politicians in the Florida legislature who voted the parents out of the textbook selection process. Then and only then will we have beat our enemy at their own game. The socialist knew that if they could infiltrate the education of our children they could brainwash generations of citizens into believing that the communist enemy is our friend. THAT is what Kruschev meant when he proclaimed that communism would defeat capitalism without ever firing a shot. He

Liberty First!

KNEW that the Marxists were already in our colleges, working their way into our elementary schools and it was only a matter of time.

What is it going to take? We as parents, grandparents must declare that our children are NOT animals. Our children are NOT fodder for experimentation. Our children are OUR CHILDREN and will not be manipulated to love government more than us. Our children are the future of this great nation and we will NOT surrender our future to ideals and programming that is Anti-American, Anti-God, and Anti-morality.

We should NOT surrender our Children. We need to take back our children, take back their education, and WE TAKE BACK the future of America. We must turn the tables, educate our children on the truth of the history and principles that make America an exceptional nation. If we do not we will become no different that Spain, Italy, or Greece and we will fall, just as they are. Our children are the future of America and the future of Liberty throughout the world.

We must teach our children that it is essential to put LIBERTY FIRST and demand that our schools do the same. If we do not, we will raise a generation of future leaders who do not know what the enemy looks like, or worse will see the enemy as our friend.

Remember that every parent is a homeschool parent no matter where the child goes to school. You must sit and teach your children the right principles and values. Get good books and read to them, make them do reports on history and on American Exceptionalism. Know what they are studying and counter the lies.

God commands parents to make teaching His truth a matter of daily life. I think we must treat the principles of Liberty the same way.

Deuteronomy 6:7-9 And thou shalt teach them diligently unto thy children, and shalt talk of them when thou sittest in thine house, and when thou walkest by the way, and when thou liest down, and when thou risest up. And thou shalt bind them for a sign upon thine hand, and they shall be as frontlets between thine eyes. And thou shalt write them upon the posts of thy house, and on thy gates.

Liberty First!

I for one will not send my young son to government schools. It is a sacrifice that our family has decided to make. I prefer my child's mind to be protected more than I need to have cable or the fanciest car or the latest gadgets. But, if your child does attend government school, you MUST protect them from brainwashing; it is your DUTY.

My first recommendation would be to homeschool them or join with some homeschool group. The second option is to find a good private school, even if you have to beg, borrow and cut out non-essentials. However, you must still supplement their education with sound teaching on the principles of Liberty. Even most private schools lack a robust "Liberty" curriculum. There are many materials that you can use, including my DVD seminar and books. The last option on the list (which I don't recommend) is government school. Just remember, you must be the monitor and the antidote to the government-sponsored brainwashing. Our children must develop into citizens who put Liberty First.

- Understand That Our Educational Problems Exist In Its Very Foundation.

- Learn The Marks of Statist, Collectivist, Humanist Propaganda.

- Counteract The Brainwashing With Right Information.

- Live And Teach Liberty First Principles Every Day.

- Take Control Of Your Child's Education.

- Remember That You Are The Parent; It is Your Duty To Educate Your Child, Not The Government's.

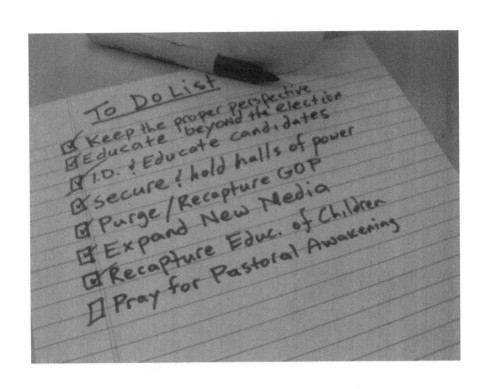

8. Pray for Pastoral Awakening

Our founders gave us a nation built on the principle of religious liberty, a nation in which the government may not coerce the citizen to believe or not believe. They envisioned a nation where the atheist and the believer alike could be free to follow the dictates of his own conscience. The founders established a nation where no man would be forced to worship and no man would be forced to be silent in his expression of faith. One of the things that has made America exceptional in the history of nations is its respect for man's religious freedom as part of the national compact. That framework was fought for primarily by those with a firm belief in God.

Our founders believed that we are endowed by our Creator with certain unalienable rights. Our founders expressed boldly and clearly that God was the source of Liberty. They believed with unwavering certainty that the Sovereign God of Divine Providence must not be abandoned nor forgotten. They declared boldly that faithful adherence to the religious principles of virtue and morality were the only sure source of securing the prosperity and continuance of this great nation.

I believe, as Benjamin Franklin did, that the hand of God was evident in the establishment of America, and our founders sought Divine guidance as they laid the foundations for America's government. In the transcript of the Constitutional Convention June 28, 1787 we find these statements from Mr. Franklin:

"In this situation of this Assembly, groping as it were in the dark to find political truth, and scarce able to distinguish it when presented to us, how has it happened, Sir, that we have not hitherto once thought of humbly applying to the Father of lights to illuminate our understandings? In the beginning of the Contest with G. Britain, when we were sensible of danger we had daily prayer in this room for the divine protection.- Our prayers, Sir, were heard, & they were graciously answered. All of us who were engaged in the struggle must have observed frequent instances of a superintending providence in our favor. To that kind providence we owe this happy

opportunity of consulting in peace on the means of establishing our future national felicity. And have we now forgotten that powerful friend? or do we imagine that we no longer need his assistance? I have lived, Sir, a long time, and the longer I live, the more convincing proofs I see of this truth- that God Governs in the affairs of men. And if a sparrow cannot fall to the ground without his notice, is it probable that an empire can rise without his aid? We have been assured, Sir, in the sacred writings, that "except the Lord build the House they labour in vain that build it." I firmly believe this; and I also believe that without his concurring aid we shall succeed in this political building no better, than the Builders of Babel: We shall be divided by our little partial local interests; our projects will be confounded, and we ourselves shall become a reproach and bye word down to future ages. And what is worse, mankind may hereafter from this unfortunate instance, despair of establishing Governments by Human wisdom and leave it to chance, war and conquest."

"I therefore beg leave to move-that henceforth prayers imploring the assistance of Heaven, and its blessings on our deliberations, be held in this Assembly every morning before we proceed to business, and that one or more of the Clergy of this City be requested to officiate in that Service."

I agree with John Adams, who stated in an address to Officers of the First Brigade of the Third Division of the Militia of Massachusetts in 1798:

"Our Constitution was made only for a moral and religious people. It is wholly inadequate to the government of any other."

I believe, as Adams did, that America's unique moral character is what would provide security for the future of the nation that the Hand of God had established :

"While our country remains untainted with the principles and manners which are now producing desolation in so many parts of the world; while she continues sincere, and incapable of insidious and impious policy, we shall have the strongest reason to rejoice in the local destination assigned us by Providence."

I believe as Thomas Jefferson did that removing God from the marketplace of government and from the minds of the people would lead directly to the loss of Liberty:

"Can the liberties of a nation be thought secure when we have removed their only firm basis, a conviction in the minds of the people that these liberties are of the gift of God? That they are not to be violated but with his wrath?"

The beliefs of our founders are made clear in nearly every original State Constitution and Charter where we find the settlers declaring that the state was being settled for the glory of God. This is plainly declared for all to see.

I agree with our first President when he declared in his Farewell address that "religious principle" is the very basis of our government and the only true source of its continued prosperity.

"Of all the dispositions and habits which lead to political prosperity, religion and morality are indispensable supports. In vain would that man claim the tribute of patriotism, who should labor to subvert these great pillars of human happiness, these firmest props

of the duties of men and citizens. The mere politician, equally with the pious man, ought to respect and to cherish them...And let us with caution indulge the supposition that morality can be maintained without religion. Whatever may be conceded to the influence of refined education on minds of peculiar structure, reason and experience both forbid us to expect that national morality can prevail in exclusion of religious principle."

"It is substantially true that virtue or morality is a necessary spring of popular government...Who that is a sincere friend to it can look with indifference upon attempts to shake the foundation of the fabric?"

It is interesting to note here that Washington suggests that those who "subvert" the duties of religion could not be called patriots – that is, that such action would be "un-American."

I could go on to quote the likes of Patrick Henry, Samuel Adams, Richard Henry Lee, John Jay and others. All of whom believed in Divine protection, provision, and providence from the

Father of Liberty – the God of Heaven and Earth. They did not shy at any level of government from boldly declaring their beliefs.

It is abundantly clear that our founders believed that America is a gift from God, Liberty is a gift from God – and "to whom much is given, much is required." We are to be faithful stewards of the gifts God has given us. In Matthew 25 Jesus teaches the parable of the talents. The immediate context seems to teach a direct application to those that were given the Word of God and were not faithful to it; but, the principle highlighted applies to ANY gift that God has entrusted to man. Two immutable truths are evident in this parable. First, that we are to prosper God's gift and second, we will be held accountable for what we do (or don't do) with what God has given us. The unfaithful servant was punished not so much for the loss of God's gift, but specifically because of inaction. The loss of the gift was the result of his inaction. It is not enough to expect someone else to do your duty. The people of God must be active in prospering, as well as protecting God's gifts – in America's case, the gift of Liberty.

Liberty First!

So if this is what our founders believed, and this is what God expects of His people, why is it that our pulpits are so quiet when it comes to the issue of Liberty? Why are our pulpits happy to decry the devastating effects of unrighteousness in every crack and crevice of society EXCEPT the "halls of power?"

Many pastors firmly assert that Christians, much less preachers, should not speak on matters of politics. Did you hear that God? You better stay out of politics; You're not allowed to go there. Of course not all pastors are silent. My husband certainly is not, neither is C.L. Bryant or Dr. Gene Youngblood and others. I thank God for those men of God who take their duty before God seriously, as did the pastors who gave us this nation.

Some of the pastors of our day do not resemble in any way the pastors alive at our founding? What would today's preachers say if they were to discover that it was a Baptist Pastor who gave us our First Amendment protections of religious Liberty?

When the first settler's came to the continent in the name of religious liberty, they established charter governments (colonies) and state religions for each charter. If you did not belong to that religion you could not legally preach or worship in that state. Since there was no Baptist charter, men like Obadiah Holmes were arrested, fined, imprisoned, and tortured for refusing to take a license to preach.

Several states, most prominently Virginia, refused to ratify the proposed Constitution because they felt: "Whether the new Federal Constitution, which had now lately made its appearance in public, made sufficient provision for the secure enjoyment of religious liberty; on which it was agreed unanimously that, in the opinion of the General Committee, it did not." ~Virginia Baptist General Convention March 7, 1788

Virginia was led in this stand by the Virginia Baptist General Convention. A Baptist Pastor, by the name of John Leland was the head of this group. Virginia wanted Pastor Leland to be the delegate for Virginia in the Constitutional Convention. Pastor Leland did not trust his own ability to be an effective delegate.

However, John Leland was a strong advocate for religious liberty.
He said,

"Every man must give account of himself to God, and therefore every man ought to be at liberty to serve God in that way that he can best reconcile it to his conscience. If government can answer for individuals at the day of judgment, let men be controlled by it in religious matters; otherwise let me be free."

John Leland met with Thomas Jefferson and James Madison and struck a deal. He offered James Madison his position as delegate for the state of Virginia as long as Madison promised that he would make sure there were sufficient protections for religious liberty; namely a Bill of Rights. Madison made his promise and held to it, being not only an ardent proponent for religious liberty, but for the entire Bill of Rights. If you are interested in a fairly good account of this agreement, you can find this story in a movie titled, Magnificent Heritage. I also recommend <u>America In Crimson Red</u> by James Beller, if you want to learn about the persecution that gave us our religious Liberty in America.

If these Christians followed the teaching of most of our modern-day pastors, America would look vastly different. We would have no First Amendment, no Bill of rights – in fact we would have no Constitution and therefore no America. I am afraid if our pastors do not reengage in there duty to stand for the gifts of God, we will achieve that very result – there will be no America.

Many pastors believe that the Bible teaches America's demise and therefore there is nothing they can or should do. My pastor/husband disagrees. Here is an excerpt from his sermon on the topic:

"It is not our place to postulate when or if America will fade from the world scene. It is simply our obligation to be faithful. God has commanded us to stand against unrighteousness and we can't say that the unrighteousness is in the government and is therefore exempt."

"God is sovereign and He does not acknowledge 'no trespassing' signs erected by man. The God of the pew is the God of politics. He expects His people to be the salt of the earth and does

not accept man's restrictions on where that salt is to be distributed. He says go into ALL the world. He declares let your light shine before men. We are to resist the Devil wherever he may be found."

"The fact is – the fascist system being foisted upon America and the world is the system of Antichrist. To submit, to not resist, is to give allegiance to that system. This battle that we are in is not a battle for America – it is a Kingdom battle. We are on a steady march toward a day when God will present mankind with one final opportunity to choose whom man will serve. It is a choice between two Kingdoms, the Kingdom of God or the Kingdom of Antichrist. Only one King will be victorious and we know Who that is. As Joshua said, 'Choose ye this day whom you will serve. As for me and my house, we will serve the Lord'."

The Bible is replete with histories of the prophets challenging leaders about unrighteousness in government. If we listen to some preachers, we should conclude that the prophets were outside of the will of God because they trespassed into an area where God is not permitted. On the contrary, it was God that gave them the message in the first place! These histories are part of the counsel of God. To ignore that and to put false boundaries around areas where truth needs to be spoken is to contradict the full counsel of God, and the consequences that affect God's people are on the hands of the spiritual leaders. (Acts 20:20-27) We must pray for a further awakening among our pastors.

My husband suggests that if you find that your church is too "cowardly" to stand for Liberty and teaches the false doctrine of isolationism in the name of Biblical separation, then you should challenge that pastor to man up or find a new church!

Pray that our pastors are not constrained by fears related to tax status but by the fear of the Lord. Pray that our pastors are not constrained by fears of offending parishioners or diminishing offerings, but would strive for eternal rewards. Pray that our churches will take up the historic role they have played in the struggle for Liberty for thousands of years . Pray that our pastors and churches will realize that *because* God gave us Liberty, we must put LIBERTY FIRST!

Liberty First!

- Liberty Is A Gift From God.

- God Gifted Us With This Nation.

- To Whom Much Is Given, Much Is Required.

- We Will Answer For Our Stewardship Of God's Gifts.

- This Is A Kingdom Battle; Make Your Allegiance Known.

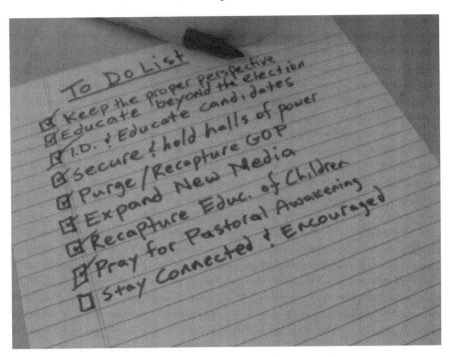

9. Stay Connected And Encouraged

If we are to sustain our fight to restore America, we must support and encourage one another. As a Christian and student of the Bible, I can tell you that the Scriptures have no shortage of teachings on the importance of fellowship and mutual support and encouragement. Hebrews 10:25 reads:

Not forsaking the assembling of ourselves together, as the manner of some is; but exhorting one another: and so much the more, as ye see the day approaching.

Conservatives do not believe in collectivism, we are individualists by nature. I, for one, have to work hard at being "social". We are often entrepreneurs, self-motivators, and believe strongly in personal responsibility. So, it is easy for us to forget that we were created to fellowship with one another. Isolationism is a dangerous state to be in. When we become isolated, we can become weakened and discouraged.

Liberty First!

I was once again reminded of the importance of unity and fellowship while attending the Right Online Conference being held by American's for Prosperity (AFP). As I mentioned, anyone who knows even a little about American's for Prosperity knows that their platform is the economic health of our nation. Who hasn't heard or seen the slogan, "It's the Spending Stupid?" But that is not why I attend. For me, the most valuable aspect of these conferences is the networking and bonding that occurs between like-minded activists. I was surprised to discover that particular benefit was not an unintended consequence. Tim Phillips, president of AFP, explained that the initial goal of AFP in having these conferences was to connect activists together and in turn connect them to the movement as a whole. Mr. Phillips explained:

"People perform better when they discover they are working for something bigger than themselves. Teams make people stronger. Even though we are individualists, we need to bond together."

The scripture I quoted also gives a timely directive, it says "so much the more, as ye see the day approaching." We are bonding together for a reason, for a bigger purpose and that purpose is approaching. We are not happy with the path this nation is on and we are angry at the destruction of Liberty perpetrated by our own government. As the days of destruction are upon us, we must not become isolated and discouraged. As the days become overwhelming, the natural instinct is to run away and go "Galt". Believe me, I know, I have fought those feelings to just stop fighting and search for that "blue pill" and reinsert into the Matrix! But we literally cannot afford to become overwhelmed - our children will suffer the most. Sam Adams wrote in the Boston Gazette in 1771:

"Let us remember that "if we suffer tamely a lawless attack upon our liberty, we encourage it, and involve others in our doom!" It is a very serious consideration, which should deeply impress our minds, that millions yet unborn may be the miserable sharers in the event!"

Liberty First!

We refuse to suffer tamely these assaults upon our Liberty, and to succeed we must remain encouraged and connected. Interestingly enough, that word encouraged literally means "to infuse with courage." The fellowship of like minds works to infuse the patriot in the home and the soldier on the field with a courage that cannot be maintained when isolated and alone. As proof of this principle, AFP tracks the activists who come to their training events. They found that activists who have bonded through the Right Online experience are three times as likely to take action locally.

We have to be a team, an army of activists with the focus our founders had - putting Liberty First to secure its "Blessings for our posterity." Mercy Otis Warren said,

"I have my fears. Yet, notwithstanding the complicated difficulties that rise before us, there is no receding...May nothing ever check that glorious spirit of freedom which inspires the patriot in the cabinet, and the hero in the field, with courage to maintain

their righteous cause, and to endeavor to transmit the claim to posterity..."

We are building an army of patriots in the cabinet and heroes in the field. Anyone who has attended military basic training knows that the most important aspect of any military corps is the loyalty to your brother in arms. Let us not be discouraged or isolated. Let us learn from each other and build each other up in mind and spirit. We are in this foxhole together, if you become discouraged and retreat, I will be left to defend this hill alone. We need to spend just as much time "infusing each other with courage" as we do battling with the enemy.

In spite of our disappointments and frustrations, we must remain resolute. Let's stay connected with one another, so that we can be infused with the courage to go forward each day. Let's stand together a strong and formidable, putting Liberty First, for the sake of our children.

Liberty First!

- Connect With Like-Minded Patriots And Groups

- Stay Hopeful

- We Didn't Get Here Overnight

- Encourage Others

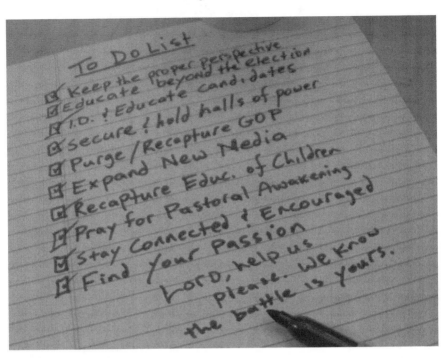

10. Find Your Passion

Finally, there are many different areas in the defense of Liberty: Freedom of Speech, Religious Liberty, Right to bear arms, Property rights etc. We probably can't devote ourselves to every cause, butwe'll fight the best for the one we are most passionate about. Find your passion and get involved. I recently was asked to teach at a conference for midwives. I make it a point to never turn down a speaking invitation, because I never know who I will reach. I am so glad that this was no exception. I met a very diverse group of men and women dedicated to their "one" aspect of Liberty; the right of woman to choose who will deliver her baby and where she will deliver. I never imagined this aspect of personal liberty was under attack. I was amazed that the people who scream that a woman is the master of her body and therefore has the "right" to abort a living child, these same people claim that a woman should not be able to choose how that baby is delivered, if she chooses to cherish that life.

Every day there are aspects of our Liberty under attack that need defending. You simply must find that thing that means so much to you that your heart quickens, your chin quivers, and your hackles stand at the thought of the government intruding upon that Liberty. You will have then found your "one thing" and you will be ready to pledge life, fortune, sacred honor.

We are a grassroots nation. Our Liberty was secured by over 700 years of grassroots movement dedicated to the inherent understanding that Liberty belongs to us and WE must secure it for our children. Our heroes must be the grassroots activists of our nation's foundation.

We must teach our sons and daughters that is was men like Sam Adams and Richard Henry Lee who picked up the mantle of their fathers and formed the Committees of Correspondence, the New Media of their time, focused upon defeating the lies disseminated by King George's Mainstream Media. It was this movement that would birth the Sons of Liberty and eventually the Boston Tea Party.

We must teach that the women were just as vocal and often more sacrificial than the men. Grassroots women like Penelope Barker who started her own movement among the women, dedicated to the boycott of Government mandated commerce and to teaching the women to be self-sufficient in the absence of their men and in defiance of their tyrannical government. Mercy Otis Warren wrote op-eds and anti-British propaganda plays and traveled the country inspiring women to do the same.

We cannot forget the original revolutionary blogger, Thomas Paine, who inspired a nation of people to maintain a steady course towards Liberty. Others like Patrick Henry, whose motivational speeches infused men to stop talking and take a stand.

I cannot forget James Otis, Jr. who took on the government in the court room and showed the people that a violation of their rights, even though justified by the government in the name of national security, was nonetheless tyranny.

Liberty First!

We began as a grassroots nation and we must believe in the power and principles of grassroots. We must pick up the mantle left before us. Grassroots, the people joined together in common cause, is the only successful solution to the problem of tyranny.

Once you have found your "one thing," follow the example of our founding activist; start a letter writing campaign; educate and inspire others to defend your "one thing"; write newspaper articles; speak at meetings; spread the truth in any way you can. We are a body in this defense of Liberty, and it is going to take all of us to restore it. Not a whole nation, but a whole body of people dedicated to the principle of Liberty First.

- Find Something That Stirs Your Passion
- Fight For It
- If Something Bothers You It Probably Bothers Others
- Search For Like-minded Groups
- Start Your Own Cause
- Be Passionate.

- People Must Not Only Hear The Argument, They Must

  Feel It.

Here is your roadmap. Now go put Liberty First!

Liberty First!

ABOUT THE AUTHOR

Fiery Advocate for the Constitution™

KrisAnne Hall is an attorney and former prosecutor, **fired after teaching the Constitution to TEA Party groups** - she would not sacrifice liberty for a paycheck. She is a disabled veteran of the US Army, a Russian linguist, a mother, a pastor's wife and a patriot. She now travels the country and teaches the Constitution and the history that gave us our founding documents.

Born and raised in St. Louis, MO. She received her undergraduate degree in Bio-Chemistry from Blackburn College in 1991 and her J.D. from the University of Florida, Levin College of Law and is a former Russian Linguist for the US Army. KrisAnne worked for several years as a state prosecutor and two years with a prominent law firm defending religious liberty and first amendment rights. KrisAnne now resides in North Florida with her husband Chris (a pastor and former foreign language instructor for the US Navy) and her adopted son Colton.

Author of Not a Living Breathing Document: Reclaiming Our Constitution, and the DVD series The Roots of Liberty: The Historic Foundations of The Bill of Rights and Bedtime Stories for Budding Patriots and Essential Stories for Junior Patriots. Two books that inspired KrisAnne's love for our history were Founding Brothers by Joseph Ellis and 1776 by David McCollough.

Awarded the Freedom Fighter award by Americans for Prosperity, the Certificate of Achievement from the Sons of the Revolution for her defense of Liberty, and Congressman James Blair Award for Defending the Constitution.

KrisAnne is an incredibly passionate speaker - a true Patrick Henry of our time. She speaks to audiences all across the country on Constitutional History, American Exceptionalism, and the Fight for Liberty. Her passion and enthusiasm is contagious and she is able to inspire any group. A steadfast warrior in the Tea Party battle. KrisAnne Hall does not just teach the Constitution, she lays the foundations that show how reliable and relevant our founding documents are today.

KrisAnne presents the **"genealogy" of the Constitution** – the 700 year history and five foundational documents that are the very roots of American Liberty.

One cannot properly understand or interpret the Constitution without a firm grasp of its very foundation.

KrisAnne will connect the dots for you like no one else can!

Nobody is teaching this. Not the 5000 year leap, not David Barton, not Heritage, not Hillsdale – yet it is essential if the Constitution is to persevere.

CONTACT HER TO SPEAK TO YOUR GROUP- FREE OF CHARGE.

The Roots of Liberty Seminar

KrisAnne Hall's "The Roots of Liberty Seminar" is NOT JUST ANOTHER LECTURE ON THE CONSTITUTION. She presents the 700+ year history that gave us our founding documents - proving that our founding documents were not created on a whim and that they are reliable and relevant. It is important to know not only what your rights are, but why you have them.

In addition to the history of the Bill of Rights, KrisAnne presents each of the first ten amendments in their context - in the words and history of our founders. She also presents the 17th amendment and what we must do to make our federal politicians accountable.

KrisAnne is a passionate speaker and has kept crowds attention for hours. This information is a must for all patriots and it must be passed on. If we are to reclaim our nation, we must reclaim our history!

Made in the USA
Middletown, DE
02 August 2015